# INTRODUCTION

To take a camera through Scotland is a daunting business. The landscape here is uncompromising in its dramatic splendour and raw beauty, and to do justice to its changing light and seasonal faces would take more than one lifetime and more than one book. Likewise this anthology of poems can only hint at the richness of expression of those Scots who have been moved to relate their lives and desires in their homes in the glens and forests and by the loch shores and the sea cliffs at the Atlantic edge of Europe. And, no less than the crofter's ruin and the drovers' roads long abandoned, these poems haunt the landscape with the voice of Columba from Iona through the Inner Isles; of Robbie Burns from the farmyards and alehouses of Galloway; of Walter Scott and Stevenson and the singers of ballads. They tell of the old Celtic gods speaking from the throat of the red deer stag and homes on the seashores, of seasons of love and harvest and kin in the kirkyard, of feuding and reiving from Borders to Highlands and Bonnie Prince Charlie and what used to be and what might have been.

I was born on the north coast of Ireland where the basalt cliffs of the Giant's Causeway face north to the Scottish islands of Jura and Islay and echo the basalt columns of Fingal's Cave in the Inner Hebrides. Over the years my work as a photographer has taken me to many beautiful places but perhaps none so beautiful to a photographer as Scotland. Although it may be overcast for a week there are shapes in the clouds and motions in the sea forever reforming their sombre hues and solid almost as the mountains. When the rain lifts there is a clearness of light which makes the colours sing. The land here teaches you patience. The moods of the weather are always changing and no view ever looks the same twice. This is a primeval landscape made for hunting. The photographer, like a stalker, sometimes has to work hard and long for a glimpse of the quarry – the fleeting conjunction of contour and light, the gift of a rainbow in a leaden sky. But well worth the wait.

The magnificent scenery of Scotland is created by the variety of rocks that lies beneath the surface, some of them amongst the very oldest of our planet's crust – the enduring gneiss and schists of the far northwest. The rifts and thrusts and erosion of the underlying rocks has determined the characters of the glens and lochs and mountains of Scotland. The more we know of what lies beneath the better we can understand and appreciate the land. Similarly, poetry and songs and stories are the layers which people have laid on top of the landscape. They tell us the lie of the land just as much as does the underpinning geology. Those who would know better the land of the Scots should read the poetry of the Scots. For those who visit Scotland for the first time and for those who already know it well, I hope this collection may throw some light on the landscape and encourage a speedy return.

**David Lyons**
*Langdale, January 1996*

# Columcille fecit

Delightful would it be to me to be in Uchd Ailiun
    On the pinnacle of a rock,
That I might often see
    The face of the ocean;
That I might see its heaving waves
    Over the wide ocean,
When they chant music to their Father
    Upon the world's course;
That I might see its level sparkling strand,
    It would be no cause of sorrow;
That I might hear the song of the wonderful birds,
    Source of happiness;
That I might hear the thunder of the crowding waves
    Upon the rocks;
That I might hear the roar by the side of the church
    Of the surrounding sea;
That I might see its noble flocks
    Over the watery ocean;
That I might see the sea-monsters,
    The greatest of all wonders;
That I might see its ebb and flood
    In their career;
That my mystical name might be, I say,
    Cul ri Erin; [1]

That contrition might come upon my heart
    Upon looking at her;
That I might bewail my evils all,
    Though it were difficult to compute them;
That I might bless the Lord
    Who conserves all,
Heaven with its countless bright orders,
    Land, strand and flood;
That I might search the books all,
    That would be good for my soul;
At times kneeling to beloved Heaven;
    At times psalm singing;
At times contemplating the King of Heaven,
    Holy the chief;
At times at work without compulsion,
    This would be delightful.
At times plucking duilisc from the rocks;
    At times at fishing;
At times giving food to the poor;
    At times in a carcair; [2]
The best advice in the presence of God
    To me has been vouchsafed.
The King whose servant I am will not let
    Anything deceive me.

*St. Columba*
*6th Century*

1 Back turned to Ireland    2 Solitary cell

# DEDICATION

For Michael Louis Calvert. Have a good trip.

This edition first published in 1996 by the
PRC Publishing Ltd,
Kiln House,
210 New Kings Road,
London SW6 4NZ.

Photographs © David Lyons 1996
Design and Layout © PRC Ltd 1996

The right of David Lyons to be identified as the author of this work
has been asserted by him in accordance with the Copyright, Designs and Patents Act 1988.

ISBN 1 85648 323 1

Printed and bound in China
Reprinted 1998

# Such a Parcel of Rogues in a Nation

Fareweel to a' our Scottish fame,
    Fareweel our ancient glory!
Fareweel ev'n to the Scottish name,
    Sae famed in martial story!
Now Sark rins o'er the Solway sands,
    An' Tweed rins to the ocean,
To mark where England's province stands –
    Such a parcel of rogues in a nation!

What force or guile could not subdue
    Thro' many warlike ages
Is wrought now by a coward few
    For hireling traitor's wages.
The English steel we could disdain,
    Secure in valour's station;
But English gold has been our bane –
    Such a parcel of rogues in a nation!

O, would, or I had seen the day
    That Treason thus could sell us,
My auld grey head had lien in clay
    Wi' Bruce and loyal Wallace!
But pith and power, till my last hour
    I'll mak this declaration;-
'We're bought and sold for English gold' –
    Such a parcel of rogues in a nation!

*Robert Burns*
*1759-1796*

# The Strange Country

I have come from a mystical Land of Light
    To a Strange Country;
The Land I have left is forgotten quite
    In the Land I see.

The round Earth rolls beneath my feet,
    And the still Stars glow,
The murmuring Waters rise and retreat,
    The Winds come and go.

Sure as a heart-beat all things seem
    In this Strange Country;
So sure, so still, in a dazzle of dream,
    All things flow free.

'Tis life, all life, be it pleasure or pain,
    In the Field and the Flood,
In the beating Heart, in the burning Brain,
    In the Flesh and the Blood.

Deep as Death is the daily strife
    Of this Strange Country:
All things thrill up till they blossom in Life,
    And flutter and flee.

Nothing is stranger than the rest,
    From the pole to the pole,
The weed by the way, the eggs in the nest,
    The Flesh and the Soul.

Look in mine eyes, O Man I meet
    In this Strange Country!
Lie in my arms, O Maiden sweet,
    With thy mouth kiss me!

Go by, O King, with thy crownèd brow
    And thy sceptred hand –
Thou art a straggler too, I vow,
    From the same strange Land.

O wondrous Faces that upstart
    In this Strange Country!
O Souls, O Shades, that become a part
    Of my Soul and me!

What are ye working so fast and fleet,
    O Humankind?
'We are building Cities for those whose feet
    Are coming behind;

'Our stay is short, we must fly again
        From this Strange Country;
But others are growing, women and men,
        Eternally!'

Child, what art thou? and what am *I*?
        But a breaking wave!
Rising and rolling on, we hie
        To the shore of the grave.

I have come from a mystical Land of Light
        To this Strange Country;
This dawn I came, I shall go to-night,
        Ay me! ay me!

I hold my hand to my head and stand
        'Neath the air's blue arc,
I try to remember the mystical Land,
        But all is dark.

And all around me swim Shapes like mine
        In this Strange Country;
They break in the glamour of gleams divine,
        And they moan 'Ay me!'

Like waves in the cold Moon's silvern breath
        They gather and roll,
Each crest of white is a birth or a death,
        Each sound is a Soul.

Oh, whose is the Eye that gleams so bright
        O'er this Strange Country?
It draws us along with a chain of light,
        As the Moon the Sea!

*Robert Buchanan*
*Born 1841*

# The Manning of the Birlinn

## The Sailing

The sun had opened golden yellow,
    From his case,
Though still the sky wore dark and drumly
    A scarr'd and frowning face:
Then troubled, tawny, dense, dun-bellied,
    Scowling and sea-blue,
Every dye that's in the tartan
    O'er it grew.
Far away to the wild westward
    Grim it lowered,
Where rain-charged clouds on thick squalls wandering
    Loomed and towered.
Up they raised the speckled sails through
    Cloud-like light,
And stretched them on the mighty halyards,
    Tense and tight.
High on the mast so tall and stately –
    Dark-red in hue –
They set them firmly, set them surely,
    Set them true.
Round the iron pegs the ropes ran,
    Each its right ring through;
Thus having ranged the tackle rarely,
    Well and carefully,
Every man sat waiting bravely,
    Where he ought to be.
For now the airy windows opened,
    And from spots of bluish grey
Let loose the keen and crabbed wild winds –
    A fierce band were they –
'Twas then his dark cloak the ocean
    Round him drew.
Dusky, livid, ruffling, whirling,
    Round at first it flew,

Till up he swell'd to mountains, or to glens,
    Dishevelled, rough, sank down –
While the kicking, tossing waters
    All in hills had grown.
Its blue depth opened in huge maws,
    Wild and devouring,
Down which, clasped in deadly struggles,
    Fierce strong waves were pouring.
It took a man to look the storm-winds
    Right in the face –
As they lit up the sparkling spray on every surge-hill,
    In their fiery race.
The waves before us, shrilly yelling,
    Raised their high heads hoar,
While those behind, with moaning trumpets,
    Gave a bellowing roar.
When we rose up aloft, majestic,
    On the heaving swell,
Need was to pull in our canvas
    Smart and well:
When she sank down with one huge swallow
    In the hollow glen,
Every sail she bore aloft
    Was given to her then.
The drizzling surges high and roaring
    Rush'd on us louting,
Long ere they were near us come,
    We heard their shouting:-
They roll'd sweeping up the little waves
    Scourging them bare,
Till all became one threatening swell,
    Our steersman's care.
When down we fell from off the billows'
    Towering shaggy edge,
Our keel was well-nigh hurled against
    The shells and sedge;
The whole sea was lashing, dashing,
    All through other:
It kept the seals and mightiest monsters
    In a pother!
The fury and the surging of the water,
    And our good ship's swift way
Spatter'd their white brains on each billow,
    Livid and grey.
With piteous wailing and complaining
    All the storm-tossed horde,
Shouted out 'We're now your subjects;
    Drag us on board.'
And the small fish of the ocean
    Turn'd over their white breast –
Dead, innumerable, with the raging
    Of the furious sea's unrest.

The stones and shells of the deep channel
    Were in motion;
Swept from out their lowly bed
    By the tumult of the ocean;
Till the sea, like a great mess of pottage,
    Troubled, muddy grew
With the blood of many mangled creatures,
    Dirty red in hue –
When the horn'd and clawy wild beasts,
    Short-footed, splay,
With great wailing gumless mouths
    Huge and wide open lay.
But the whole deep was full of spectres,
    Loose and sprawling
With the claws and with the tails of monsters,
    Pawing, squalling.
It was frightful even to hear them
    Screech so loudly;
The sound might move full fifty heroes
    Stepping proudly.
Our whole crew grew dull of hearing
    In the tempest's scowl,
So sharp the quavering cries of demons
    And the wild beasts' howl.
With the oaken planks the weltering waves were wrestling
    In their noisy splashing;

While the sharp beak of our swift ship
    On the sea-pigs came dashing.
The wind kept still renewing all its wildness
    In the far West,
Till with every kind of strain and trouble
    We were sore distress'd.
We were blinded with the water
    Showering o'er us ever;
And the awful night like thunder,
    And the lightning ceasing never.
The bright fireballs in our tackling
    Flamed and smoked;
With the smell of burning brimstone
    We were well-nigh choked.
All the elements above, below,
    Against us wrought;
Earth and wind and fire and water,
    With us fought.
But when the evil one defied the sea
    To make us yield,
At last, with one bright smile of pity,
    Peace with us she seal'd:
Yet not before our yards were injured,
    And our sails were rent,
Our poops were strained, our oars were weaken'd,
    All our masts were bent.

Not a stay but we had started,
　　Our tackling all was wet and splashy,
Nails and couplings, twisted, broken.
　　Feeshie, fashie,
All the thwarts and all the gunwale
　　Everywhere confess'd,
And all above and all below,
　　How sore they had been press'd.
Not a bracket, not a rib,
　　But the storm had loosed;
Fore and aft from stem to stern,
　　All had got confused.
Not a tiller but was split,
　　And the helm was wounded;
Every board its own complaint
　　Sadly sounded.
Every trennel, every fastening
　　Had been giving way;
Not a board remain'd as firm
　　As at the break of day.
Not a bolt in her but started,
　　Not a rope the wind that bore,
Not a part of the whole vessel
　　But was weaker than before.
The sea spoke to us its peace prattle
　　At the cross of Islay's Kyle,
And the rough wind, bitter boaster!
　　Was restrained for one good while.

The tempest rose from off us into places
　　Lofty in the upper air,
And after all its noisy barking
　　Ruffled round us fair.
Then we gave thanks to the High King,
　　Who rein'd the wind's rude breath,
And saved our good Clan Ranald
　　From a bad and brutal death.
Then we furl'd up the fine and speckled sails
　　Of linen wide,
And we took down the smooth red dainty masts,
　　And laid them by the side –
On our long and slender polish'd oars
　　Together leaning –
They were all made of the fir cut by Mac Barais
　　In Eilean Fionain –
We went with our smooth, dashing rowing,
　　And steady shock,
Till we reach'd the good port round the point
　　Of Fergus' Rock.
There casting anchor peacefully
　　We calmly rode;
We got meat and drink in plenty,
　　And there we abode.

*Alexander MacDonald*
*c.1700-1770*

# The Twa Corbies

As I was walking all alane,
I heard twa corbies making a mane; [1]
The tane[2] unto the t'other say,
'Where sall we gang[3] and dine to-day?'

'In behint yon auld fail dyke,[4]
I wot there lies a new slain knight;
And naebody kens that he lies there,
But his hawk, his hound, and lady fair.

'His hound is to the hunting gane,
His hawk to fetch the wild-fowl hame,
His lady's ta'en another mate,
So we may mak our dinner sweet.

'Ye'll sit on his white hause-bane,[5]
And I'll pike out his bonny blue een;
Wi ae lock o his gowden hair
We'll theek our nest when it grows bare.

'Mony a one for him makes mane,
But nane sall ken where he is gane;
Oer his white banes, when they are bare,
The wind sall blaw for evermair.'

*Anon*

1 moan       4 turf wall
2 the one    5 neck bone
3 go

11

# Mountain Twilight

The hills slipped over each on each
    Till all their changing shadows died.
Now in the open skyward reach
    The lights grow solemn side by side.
While of these hills the westermost
Rears high his majesty of coast
    In shifting waste of dim-blue brine
    And fading olive hyaline;
Till all the distance overflows,
    The green in watchet and the blue
In purple. Now they fuse and close –
    A darkling violet, fringed anew
With light that on the mountains soar,
A dusky flame on tranquil shores;
    Kindling the summits as they grow
In audience to the skies that call,
Ineffable in rest and all
    The pathos of the afterglow.

*William Renton*
*19th Century*

# Requiem

Under the wide and starry sky
Dig the grave and let me lie:
Glad did I live and gladly die,
    And I laid me down with a will.

This be the verse you grave for me:
*Here he lies where he long'd to be;*
*Home is the sailor, home from sea,*
    *And the hunter home from the hill.*

*Robert Louis Stevenson*
*1850-1894*

# Lock the Door, Lariston

'Lock the door, Lariston, lion of Liddesdale;
Lock the door, Lariston, Lowther comes on;
    The Armstrongs are flying,
    The widows are crying'
The Castletown's burning, and Oliver's gone!

'Lock the door, Lariston - high on the weather gleam
See how the Saxon plumes bob on the sky -
    Yeomen and carbineer,
    Billman and halberdier,
Fierce is the foray, and far is the cry!

'Bewcastle brandishes high his broad scimitar;
Ridley is riding his fleet-footed grey;
    Hedley and Howard there,
    Wandale and Windermere;
Lock the door, Lariston; hold them at bay.

'Why dost thou smile, noble Elliot of Lariston?
Why does the joy-candle gleam in thine eye?
    Thou bold Border ranger,
    Beware of thy danger;
Thy foes are relentless, determined, and nigh.'

Jack Elliot raised up his steel bonnet and lookit,
His hand grasp'd the sword with a nervous embrace;
    'Ah, welcome, brave foemen,
    On earth there are no men
More gallant to meet in the foray or chase!

'Little know you of the hearts I have hidden here;
Little know you of our moss-troopers' might -
    Linhope and Sorbie true,
    Sundhope and Milburn too,
Gentle in manner, but lions in fight!

'I have Mangerton, Ogilvie, Raeburn, and Netherbie,
Old Sim of Whitram, and all his array;
    Come all Northumberland,
    Teesdale and Cumberland,
Here at the Breaken tower end shall the fray!'

Scowled the broad sun o'er the links of green Liddesdale,
Red as the beacon-light tipped he the wold;
    Many a bold martial eye
    Mirror'd that morning sky,
Never more oped on his orbit of gold.

Shrill was the bugle's note, dreadful the warrior's shout,
Lances and halberds in splinters were borne;
    Helmet and hauberk then
    Braved the claymore in vain,
Buckler and armlet in shivers were shorn.

See how they wane - the proud files of the Windermere!
Howard! ah, woe to thy hopes of the day!
    Hear the wide welkin rend,
    While the Scots' shouts ascend -
'Elliot of Lariston, Elliot for aye!'

*James Hogg*
*1770-1835*

# Lochinvar

O, young Lochinvar is come out of the west,
Through all the wide Border his steed was the best;
And save his good broadsword he weapons had none,
He rode all unarm'd, and he rode all alone.
So faithful in love, and so dauntless in war,
There never was knight like the young Lochinvar.

He staid not for brake, and he stopp'd not for stone,
He swam the Eske river where ford there was none;
But ere he alighted at Netherby gate,
The bride had consented, the gallant came late:
For a laggard in love, and a dastard in war,
Was to wed the fair Ellen of brave Lochinvar.

So boldly he enter'd the Netherby Hall,
Among bride's-men, and kinsmen, and brothers, and all:
Then spoke the bride's father, his hand on his sword,
(For the poor craven bridegroom said never a word,)
'O come ye in peace here, or come ye in war,
Or to dance at our bridal, young Lord Lochinvar?'

'I long woo'd your daughter, my suit you denied; -
Love swells like the Solway, but ebbs like its tide -
And now am I come, with this lost love of mine,
To lead but one measure, drink one cup of wine.
There are maidens in Scotland more lovely by far,
That would gladly be bride to the young Lochinvar.'

The bride kiss'd the goblet; the knight took it up,
He quaff'd off the wine, and he threw down the cup.
She look'd down to blush, and she look'd up to sigh,
With a smile on her kips, and a tear in her eye.
He took her soft hand, ere her mother could bar, -
'Now tread we a measure!' said young Lochinvar.

So stately his form, and so lovely her face,
That never a hall such a galliard did grace;
While her mother did fret, and her father did fume,
And the bridegroom stood dangling his bonnet and plume;
And the bride-maidens whisper'd, 'Twere better by far,
To have match'd our fair cousin with young Lochinvar.'

One touch to her hand, and one word in her ear,
When they reach'd the hall-door, and the charger stood near;
So light to the croupe the fair lady he swung,
So light to the saddle before her he sprung!
'She is won! we are gone, over bank, bush, and scaur;
They'll have fleet steeds that follow,' quoth young Lochinvar.


There was mounting 'mong Graemes of the Netherby clan;
Forsters, Fenwicks, and Musgraves, they rode and they ran:
There was racing and chasing on Cannobie Lee,
But the lost bride of Netherby ne'er did they see.
So daring in love, and so dauntless in war,
Have ye e'er heard of gallant like young Lochinvar?

*Sir Walter Scott*
*1771-1832*

# Arran

Arran of the many stags,
the sea reaches to its shoulder;
island where companies are fed,
ridges whereon blue spears are reddened.

Wanton deer upon its peaks,
Mellow blaeberries on its heaths,
cold water in its streams,
mast upon its brown oaks.

Hunting dogs there, and hounds,
blackberries and sloes of the dark blackthorn,
dense thorn-bushes in its woods,
stags astray among its oak-groves.

Gathering of purple lichen on its rocks,
grass without blemish on its slopes;
over its fair shapely crags
gambolling of dappled fawns leaping.

Smooth is its lowland, fat are its swine,
pleasant its fields, a tale to be believed;
its nuts on the boughs of its hazel-wood,
sailing of long galleys past it.

It is delightful when fine weather comes,
trout under the banks of its streams,
seagulls answer each other round its white cliff;
delightful at all times is Arran.

*Anon, translated from the Irish by Kenneth Jackson*

# His Metrical Prayer
## (On the Eve of his Own Execution)

Let them bestow on ev'ry Airth[1] a Limb;
Open all my veins, that I may swim
To Thee my Saviour, in that Crimson Lake;
Then place my par-boiled Head upon a Stake;
Scatter my Ashes, throw them in the Air:
Lord (since Thou know'st where all these Atoms are)
I'm hopeful, once Thou'lt recollect my Dust,
And confident Thou'lt raise me with the Just.

*James Graham*
*Marquis of Montrose*
*1612-1650*

[1] north, south, east and west

# In Shadowland

Between the moaning of the mountain stream
And the hoarse thunder of the Atlantic deep,
An outcast from the peaceful realms of sleep
I lie, and hear as in a fever-dream
The homeless night-wind in the darkness scream
And wail around the inaccessible steep
Down whose gaunt sides the spectral torrents leap
From crag to crag, - till almost I could deem
The plaided ghosts of buried centuries
Were mustering in the glen with bow and spear
And shadowy hounds to hunt the shadowy deer,
Mix in phantasmal sword-play, or, with eyes
Of wrath and pain immortal, wander o'er
Loved scenes where human footstep comes no more.

*Sir Noel Paton*
*Born 1821*

# The Reed-Player

By a dim shore where water darkening
    Took the last light of spring,
I went beyond the tumult, harkening
    For some diviner thing.

Where the bats flew from the black elms like leaves,
    Over the ebon pool
Brooded the bittern's cry, as one that grieves
    Lands ancient, bountiful.

I saw the fire-flies shine below the wood,
    Above the shallows dank,
As Uriel, from some great altitude,
    The planets rank on rank.

And now unseen along the shrouded mead
    One went under the hill;
He blew a cadence on his mellow reed,
    That trembled and was still.

It seemed as if a line of amber fire
    Had shot the gathered dusk,
As if had blown a wind from ancient Tyre
    Laden with myrrh and musk.

He gave his luring note amid the fern;
    Its enigmatic fall
Haunted the hollow dusk with golden turn
    And argent interval.

I could not know the message that he bore,
    The springs of life from me
Hidden; his incommunicable lore
    As much a mystery.

And as I followed far the magic player
    He passed the maple wood;
And, when I passed, the stars had risen there,
    And there was solitude.

*Duncan Campbell-Scott*
*19th Century*

# Venus and Cupid

Frae bank to bank, frae wood to wood I rin
Owrhailit[1] with my feeble fantasie,
Like til a leaf that fallis from a tree,
Or til a reed owrblawin with the wind.
Twa gods guides me: the ane of them is blin,
Yea, and a bairn brocht up in vanitie;
The nixt a wife ingenerit[2] of the sea
And lichter nor a dauphin[3] with her fin.

Unhappie is the man for evermair
That tills the sand and sawis in the air;
But twice unhappier is he, I lairn,
That feedis in his hairt a mad desire,
And follows on a woman throu the fire,
Led by a blin, and teachit by a bairn.

*Mark Alexander Boyd*
*1563-1601*

1  overwhelmed
2 born of
3  dolphin

# The wee, wee German Lairdie

Wha the deil hae we got for a King,
    But a wee, wee German lairdie![1]
An' whan we gaed to bring him hame,
    He was delving in his kail-yardie.[2]
Sheughing[3] kail an' laying leeks,
    But[4] the hose and but the breeks,
Up his beggar duds[5] he cleeks,
    The wee, wee German lairdie.

An' he's clapt down in our gudeman's[6] chair,
    The wee, wee German lairdie;
An' he's brought fouth[7] o' foreign leeks,
    An' dibblet them in his yardie.
He's pu'd the rose o' English louns,[8]
    An' brak the harp o' Irish clowns,
But our thistle will jag his thumbs,
    The wee, wee German lairdie.

Come up amang the Highland hills,
    Thou wee, wee German lairdie;
An' see how Charlie's lang-kail[9] thrive,
    He dibblet in his yardie.
An' if a stock ye daur[10] to pu',
    Or haud[11] the yoking of a pleugh,
We'll break yere sceptre o'er yere mou',
    Thou wee bit German lairdie.

Our hills are steep, our glens are deep,
    Nae fitting for a yardie;
An' our norlan' thistles winna pu'
    Thou wee, wee German lairdie.
An' we've the trenching blades o' weir,[12]
    Wad twine ye o' yere German gear
An' pass ye 'neath the claymore's shear,
    Thou feckless[13] German lairdie.

| | | | |
|---|---|---|---|
| 1 minor squire | 5 rags | 9 swords of Prince | 12 war |
| 2 cabbage patch | 6 king | Charles Edward's men | 13 useless |
| 3 picking | 7 many | 10 dare | |
| 4 without | 8 fellows | 11 hold | |

*Allan Cunningham*
*1784-1842*

# To His Mistress

So sweet a kiss yestreen frae thee I reft,
In bowing doun thy body on the bed,
That even my life within thy lips I left.
Sensyne[1] from thee my spirits wald never shed.
To follow thee it from my body fled
And left my corpse als cold as ony key.
But when the danger of my death I dread,
To seek my spreit I sent by hairt to thee;
But it was so enamoured with thine ee,
With thee it mindit likewise to remain.
So thou hes keepit captive all the three,
More glaid to bide than to return again.
    Except thy breath their places had suppleit,
    Even in thine armes, there doutless had I deit.

*Alexander Montgomerie*
*c.1545-c.1610*

1  since then

# The Hill-Water

From the rim it trickles down
Of the mountains granite crown clear and cool;
Keen and eager though it go
Through your veins with lively flow,
Yet it knoweth not to reign
In the chambers of the brain with misrule;

Where dark watercresses grow
You will trace its quiet flow,
With mossy border yellow,
So mild and soft, and mellow, in its pouring.
With no shiny dregs to trouble
The brightness of its bubble
As it threads its silver way
From the granite shoulders grey of Ben Dorain.

Then down the sloping side
It will leap with glassy slide gently welling
Till it gather strength to leap,
With a light and foamy sweep,
To the corrie broad and deep
Proudly swelling;

Then bends amid the boulders
'Neath the shadow of the shoulders of the Ben,
Through a country rough and shaggy,
So jaggy and so knaggy,
Full of hummocks and of hunches,
Full of stumps and tufts and bunches,
Full of bushes and of rushes, in the glen,

Through rich green solitudes,
And wildly hanging woods
With blossom and with bell,
In rich redundant swell, and the pride
Of the mountain daisy there, and the forest everywhere,
With the dress and with the air of a bride.

*Duncan Ban MacIntyre*
*1724-1808*

# McLean's Welcome

Come o'er the stream, Charlie, dear Charlie, brave Charlie;
Come o'er the stream, Charlie, and dine with McLean;
And though you be weary, we'll make you heart cheery,
And welcome our Charlie, and his loyal train.
We'll bring down the track deer, we'll bring down the black steer,
The lamb from the braken, and doe from the glen,
The salt sea we'll harry, and bring to our Charlie
The cream from the bothy and curd from the pen.

Come o'er the stream, Charlie, dear Charlie, brave Charlie;
Come o'er the stream, Charlie, and dine with McLean;
And you shall drink freely the dews of Glen-Sheerly,
That stream in the starlight when kings do not ken,
And deep be your meed of the wine that is red,
To drink to your sire, and his friend the McLean.

Come o'er the stream, Charlie, dear Charlie, brave Charlie;
Come o'er the stream, Charlie, and dine with McLean;
O'er heath-bells shall trace you the maids to embrace you,
And deck your blue bonnet with flowers of the brae;
And the loveliest Mari in all Glen M'Quarry
Shall lie in your bosom till break of the day.

Come o'er the stream, Charlie, dear Charlie, brave Charlie;
Come o'er the stream, Charlie, and dine with McLean;
If aught will invite you, or more will delight you,
'Tis ready, a troop of our bold Highlandmen,
All ranged on the heather, with bonnet and feather,
Strong arms and broad claymores, three hundred and ten!

*James Hogg*
*1770-1835*

# Scots, Wha Hae

Scots, wha hae wi'[1] Wallace bled,
Scots, wham Bruce has aften[2] led,
Welcome to your gory bed
    Or to victorie!

Now's the day, and now's the hour:
See the front o' battle lour,[3]
See approach proud Edward's power -
    Chains and slaverie!

Wha will be a traitor knave?
Wha can fill a coward's grave?
Wha sae base as be a slave?
    Let him turn and flee!

Wha for Scotland's King and Law
Freedom's sword will strongly draw,
Freeman stand, or freeman fa',
    Let him follow me!

By Oppression's woes and pains,
By your sons in servile chains,
We will drain our dearest veins
    But they shall be free!

Lay the proud usurpers low!
Tyrants fall in every foe!
Liberty's in every blow!
    Let us do, or die!

1 who have with
2 often
3 loom up

*Robert Burns 1759-1796*

# The Lament of the Deer
## (Cumha nam Fiadh)

O for my strength! once more to see the hills!
The wilds of Strath-Farar of stags,
The blue streams, and winding vales,
Where the flowering tree sends forth its sweet perfume.

My thoughts are sad and dark! -
I lament the forest where I loved to roam,
The secret corries, the haunt of hinds,
Where often I watched them on the hill!

Corrie-Garave! O that I was within thy bosom
Scuir-na-Lapàich of steeps, with thy shelter,
Where feed the herds which never seek for stalls,
But whose skin gleams red in the sunshine of the hills.

Great was my love in youth, and strong my desire,
Towards the bounding herds;
But now, broken, and weak, and hopeless,
Their remembrance wounds my heart.

To linger in the laich[1] I mourn,
My thoughts are ever in the hills;
For there my childhood and my youth was nursed -
The moss and the craig in the morning breeze was my delight.

Then was I happy in my life,
When the voices of the hill sung sweetly;
More sweet to me, than any string,
It soothed my sorrow or rejoiced my heart.

My thoughts wandered to no other land
Beyond the hill of the forest, the shealings of the deer,
Where the nimble herds ascended the hill, -
As I lay in my plaid on the dewy bed.

The sheltering hollows, where I crept towards the hart,
On the pastures of the glen, or in the forest wilds -
And if once more I may see them as of old,
How will my heart bound to watch again the pass!

Great was my joy to ascend the hills
In the cause of the noble chief,
Mac Shimé of the piercing eye - never to fail at need,
With all his brave Frasers, gathered beneath his banner.

When they told of his approach, with all his ready arms,
My heart bounded for the chase -
On the rugged steep, on the broken hill,
By hollow, and ridge, many were the red stags which he laid low.

He is the pride of hunters; my trust was in his gun,
When the sound of its shot rung in my ear,
The great ball launched in flashing fire,
And the dun stag fell in the rushing speed of his course.

When evening came down on the hill,
The time for return to the star of the glen,
The kindly lodge where the noble gathered,
The sons of the tartan and the plaid,

With joy and triumph they returned
To the dwelling of plenty and repose;
The bright blazing hearth - the circling wine -
The welcome of the noble chief!

1  Low country

*Angus MacKenzie*
*published 1848*

# O my luve's like a red, red rose

O my luve's like a red, red rose,
    That's newly sprung in June:
O my luve's like the melodie
    That's sweetly play'd in tune.

As fair art thou, my bonnie lass,
    So deep in luve am I;
And I will luve thee still, my dear,
    Till a' the seas gang dry.

Till a' the seas gang dry, my dear,
    And the rocks will melt wi' the sun;
And I will luve thee still, my dear,
    While the sands o' life shall run.

And fare thee weel, my only luve!
    And fare thee weel a while!
And I will come again, my luve,
    Tho' it were ten thousand mile.

*Robert Burns*
*1759-1796*

# Durisdeer

We'll meet nae mair at sunset when the weary day is dune,
Nor wander hame thegither by the lee licht o' the mune.
I'll hear your steps nea langer amang the dewy corn,
For we'll meet nae mair, my bonniest, either at e'en or morn.

The yellow broom is waving abune the sunny brae,
And the rowan berries dancing where the sparkling waters play;
Tho' a' is bright and bonnie it's an eerie place to me,
For we'll meet nae mair, my dearest, either by burn or tree.

Far up into the wild hills there's a kirkyard lone and still,
Where the frosts lie ilka morning and the mists hang low and chill.
And there ye sleep in silence while I wander here my lane
Till we meet ance mair in Heaven never to part again!

*Lady John Scott*
*19th Century*

# Thomas the Rhymer

True Thomas lay on Huntlie bank;
    A ferlie he spied wi' his e'e;
And there he saw a ladye bright
    Come riding down by the Eildon Tree.


Her skirt was o' the grass-green silk,
    Her mantle o' the velvet fyne;
At ilka tett o' her horse's mane
    Hung fifty siller bells and nine.


True Thomas he pu'd aff his cap,
    And louted low down on his knee:
'Hail to thee, Mary, Queen of Heaven!
    For thy peer on earth could never be.'


'O no, O no, Thomas,' she said
    'That name does not belang to me;
I'm but the Queen o' fair Elfland,
    That am hither come to visit thee.

'Harp and carp, Thomas,' she said;
    'Harp and carp along wi' me;
And if ye dare to kiss my lips,
    Sure of your bodie I will be.'

'Betide me weal, betide me woe,
    That weird shall never daunten me.'
Syne he has kiss'd her rosy lips,
    All underneath the Eildon Tree.


'Now ye maun go wi' me,' she said,
    'True Thomas, ye maun go wi' me;
And ye maun serve me seven years,
    Thro' weal or woe as may chance to be.'


She's mounted on her milk-white steed,
    She's ta'en true Thomas up behind;
And aye, whene'er her bridle rang,
    The steed gaed swifter that the wind.


O they rade on, and farther on,
    The steed gaed swifter than the wind;
Until they reach'd a desert wide,
    And living land was left behind.


'Light down, light down now, true Thomas,
    And lean your head upon my knee;
Abide ye there a little space,
    And I will show you ferlies three.

'O see ye not yon narrow road,
        So thick beset wi' thorns and briers?
That is the Path of Righteousness,
        Though after it but few inquires.

'And see ye not yon braid, braid road,
        That lies across the lily leven?
That is the Path of Wickedness,
        Though some call it the Road to Heaven.

'And see ye not yon bonny road
        That winds about the fernie brae?
That is the road to fair Elfland,
        Where thou and I this night might maun
                                    gae.

'But, Thomas, ye sall haud your tongue,
        Whatever ye may hear or see;
For speak ye word in Elfyn-land,
        Ye'll ne'er win back to your ain countrie.'

O they rade on, and farther on,
        And they waded river abune the knee;
And they saw neither sun nor moon,
        But they heard the roaring of the sea.

It was mirk, mirk night, there was nae starlight,
        They waded thro' red blude to the knee;
For a' the blude that's shed on the earth
        Rins through the springs o' that countrie.

Syne they came to a garden green,
        And she pu'd an apple frae a tree:
'Take this for thy wages, true Thomas;
        It will give thee the tongue that can never lee.'

'My tongue us my ain,' true Thomas he said;
        'A gudely gift ye wad gie to me!
I neither dought to buy or sell
        At fair or tryst where I might be.

'I  dought neither speak to prince or peer,
        Nor ask of grace from fair ladye!' -
'Now haud thy peace, Thomas,'she said,
        "For as I say, so must it be.'

He has gotten a coat of even cloth,
        And a pair o' shoon of the velvet green;
And till seven years were gane and past,
        True Thomas on earth was never seen.

*Anonymous*

# The Hind is in the Forest

The hind is in the forest
as she ought to be,
where she may have sweet grass,
clean, fine-bladed;
    heath-rush and deer's hair grass
    herbs in which strength resides,
    and which would make her flanks
    plump and fat-covered;
    a spring in which there is
    adundant water-cress,
    she deems more sweet than wine,
    and would drink of it;
    sorrel and rye grass
    which flourish on the moor,
    she prefers as food
    to rank field grass.

Of her fare she deemed
these the delicacies:
primrose, St John's wort
and tormentil flowers;
    tender spotted orchis,
    forked, spiked and glossy,
    on meadows where, in clusters,
    it flourishes.
    Such was the dietary
    that would increase their strength,
    that would pull them through
    in the stormy days;
    that would upon their back
    amass the roll of fat,
    which, over their spare frame,
    was not cumbersome.

That was a comely fellowship
at eventide,
when they would assemble
in the gloaming:
    though long the night might be
    no harm would come to you;
    the lee base of the knoll
    was your dwelling place.
    Here are the beds of deer,
    where they have ever been,
    on a spacious, bounteous moor,
    and on  mountain range.
    Delightful was their hue,
    when vivid was their hide;
    'twas no mean portion they desired,
    it was Ben Dobhrain.

*Duncan Ban MacIntyre*
*1724-1808*

# To S. R. Crockett
## (On receiving a Dedication)

Blows the wind today, and the sun and the rain are flying,
    Blows the wind on the moors today and now,
Where about the graves of the martyrs the whaups[1] are crying,
    My heart remembers how!

Grey recumbent tombs of the dead in desert places,
    Standing-stones on the vacant wine-red moor,
Hills of sheep, and the howes[2] of the silent vanished races,
    And winds, austere and pure.

Be it granted me to behold you again in dying,
    Hills of home! and to hear again the call;
Hear about the graves of the martyrs the peewees[3] crying,
    And hear no more at all.

*Robert Louis Stevenson*
*1850-1894*

1  curlews
2  hollows, glens
3  lapwings

# The Highland Crofter

Frae Kenmore tae Ben More
The land is a' the Marquis's;
The mossy howes, the heathery knowes
An' ilka bonnie park is his;
The bearded goats, the towsie stots,
An' a' the braxie carcases;
Ilk crofter's rent, ilk tinkler's tent,
An ilka collie's bark is his;
The muir-cock's craw, the piper's blaw,
The ghillie's hard day's wark is his;
Frae Kenmore tae Ben More
The warld is a' the Marquis's.

The fish that swim, the birds that skim,
The fir, the ash, the birk is his;
The Castle ha' sae big and braw,
Yon diamond-crusted dirk is his;
The roofless hame, a burning shame,

The factor's dirty wark is his;
The poor folk vexed, the lawyer's text,
Yon smirking legal shark is his;
Frae Kenmore tae Ben More
The warld is a' the Marquis's.
But near, mair near, God's voice we hear -
The dawn as weel's the dark is His;
The poet's dream, the patriot's theme,
The fire that lights the mirk is His.
They clearly show God's mills are slow
But sure the handiwork is His;
And in His grace our hope we place;
Fair Freedom's sheltering ark is His.
The men that toil should own the soil -
A note as clear's the lark is this -
Breadalbane's land - the fair, the grand -
Will no' be aye the Marquis's.

*Anonymous*

# The Last Journey
## (From *The Testament of John Davidson*)

I felt the world a-spinning on its nave,
    I felt it sheering blindly round the sun;
I felt the time had come to find a grave:
    I knew it in my heart my days were done.
I took my staff in hand; I took the road,
And wandered out to seek my last abode.
        Hearts of gold and hearts of lead
        Sing it yet in sun and rain
        'Heel and toe from dawn to dusk,
        Round the world and home again.'

O long before the bere was steeped for malt,
    And long before the grape was crushed for wine,
The glory of the march without a halt,
    The triumph of a stride like yours and mine
Was known to folk like us, who walked about,
To be the sprightliest cordial out and out!
        Folk like us, with hearts that beat
        Sang it too in sun and rain
        'Heel and toe from dawn to dusk,
        Round the world and home again.'

My feet are heavy now, but on I go,
    My head erect beneath the tragic years.
The way is steep, but I would have it so;
    And dusty, but I lay the dust with tears,
Though none can see me weep: alone I climb
The rugged path that leads me out of time -
        Out of time and out of all,
        Singing yet in sun and rain
        'Heel and toe from dawn to dusk,
        Round the world and home again.'

Farewell the hope that mocked, farewell despair
    That went before me still and made the pace.
The earth is full of graves, and mine was there
    Before my life began, my resting-place;
And I shall find it out and with the dead
Lie down for ever, all my sayings said -
        Deeds all done and songs all sung,
        While others chant in sun and rain,
        'Heel and toe from dawn to dusk,
        Round the world and home again.'

*John Davidson*
*1857-1909*

# The Tryst

O luely, luely, cam she in
And luely she lay doun:
I kent her be her caller lips
And her briests sae sma' and roun'.

A' thru the nicht we spak nae word
Nor sinder'd bane frae bane:
A' thru the nicht I heard her hert
Gang soundin' wi' my ain.

It was about the waukrife hour
Whan cocks begin to craw
That she smool'd saftly thru the mirk
Afore the day wud daw.

Sae luely, luely, cam she in
Sae luely was she gaen;
And wi' her a' my simmer days
Like they had never been.

*William Soutar*
*1898-1943*

# Bonny Kilmeny gaed up the Glen

Bonny Kilmeny gaed up the glen,
But it wasna to meet Duneira's men,
Nor the rosy monk on the isle to see,
For Kilmeny was pure as pure could be.
It was only to hear the yorlin sing,
And pu' the cress-flower round the spring;
The scarlet hypp and the hindberrye,
And the nut that hung frae the hazel tree;
For Kilmeny was as pure as pure could be.
But lang may her minny look o'er the wa',
And lang may she seek i' the green-wood shaw;
Lang the laird of Duneira blame,
And lang, lang greet or Kilmeny come hame!

When many a day had come and fled,
When grief grew calm, and hope was dead,
When mass for Kilmeny's soul had been sung,
When the bedes-man had prayed, and the dead bell rung,
Late, late in a gloamin' when all was still,

When the fringe was red on the westlin hill,
The wood was sere, the moon i' the wane,
The reek o' the cot hung over the plain,
Like a little wee cloud in the world its lane;
When the ingle lowed with an eiry leme,
Late, late in the gloamin' Kilmeny came hame!
'Kilmeny, Kilmeny, where have you been?
Lang hae we sought baith holt and dean;
By linn, by ford, and green-wood tree,
Yet you are halesome and fair to see.
Where gat you that joup o' the lily schene?
That bonny snood of the birk sae green?
And these roses, the fairest that ever were seen?
Kilmeny, Kilmeny, where have you been?'

Kilmeny looked up with a lovely grace,
But nae smile was seen on Kilmeny's face;
As still was her look, and as still was her ee,
As the stillness that lay on the emerant lea,

Or the mist that sleeps on a waveless sea.
For Kilmeny had been she knew not where,
And Kilmeny had seen what she could not declare;
Kilmeny had been where the cock never crew,
Where the rain never fell, and the wind never blew;
But it seemed as the harp of the sky had rung,
And the airs of heaven played round her tongue,
When she spake of the lovely forms she had seen,
And a land where sin had never been;
A land of love, and a land of light,
Withouten sun, or moon, or night;
Where the river swa'd a living stream,
And the light a pure celestial beam:
The land of vision it would seem,
A still, an everlasting dream...
When seven lang years had come and fled;
When grief was calm, and hope was dead;
When scarce was remembered Kilmeny's name,
Late, late in a gloamin' Kilmeny came hame!

*James Hogg*
*1770-1835*

# Skye

My heart is yearning to thee, O Skye!
    Dearest of Islands!
There first the sunshine gladdened my eye,
    On the sea sparkling;
There doth the dust of my dear ones lie,
    In the old graveyard.

Bright are the golden green fields to me,
    Here in the Lowlands;
Sweet sings the mavis in the thorn-tree,
    Snowy with fragrance:
But oh for a breath of the great North Sea,
    Girdling the mountains!

Good is the smell of the brine that laves
    Black rock and skerry,
Where the great palm-leaved tangle waves
    Down in the green depths,
And round the craggy bluff pierced with caves
    Sea-gulls are screaming.

When the sun sinks below Humish Head,
    Crowning in glory,
As he goes down to his ocean bed
    Studded with islands,
Flushing the Coolin with royal red,
    Would I were sailing!

Many a hearth round that friendly shore
    Giveth warm welcome;
Charms still are there, as in days of yore,
    More than of mountains;
But hearths and faces are seen no more
    Once of the brightest.

Many a poor black cottage is there,
    Grimy with peat smoke,
Sending up in the soft evening air
    Purest blue incense,
While the low music of psalm and prayer
    Rises to Heaven.

Kind were the voices I used to hear
    Round such a fireside,
Speaking the mother tongue old and dear,
    Making the heart beat
With sudden tales of wonder and fear,
    Or plaintive singing.

Reared in those dwellings have brave ones been;
    Brave ones are still there;
Forth from their darkness on Sunday I've seen
    Coming pure linen,
And like the linen the souls were clean
    Of them that wore it.

See that thou kindly use them, O man!
    To whom God giveth
Stewardship over them, in thy short span
    Not for thy pleasure;
Woe be to them who choose for a clan
    Four-footed people!

Great were the marvellous stories told
    Of Ossian's heroes,
Giants, and witches, and young men bold,
    Seeking adventures,
Winning kings' daughters and guarded gold,
    Only with valour.

Blessings be with ye, both now and aye
    Dear human creatures!
Yours is the love that no gold can buy!
    Nor time wither
Peace be to thee and thy children, O Skye!
    Dearest of islands.

*Alexander Nicolson*
*19th Century*

# Canadian Boat Song

Fair these broad meads - these hoary woods are grand;
    But we are exiles from our fathers' land.

Listen to me, as when ye heard our father
    Sing long ago the song of other shores -
Listen to me, and then in chorus gather
    All your deep voices, as ye pull your oars.

From the lone shieling[1] of the misty island
    Mountains divide us, and waste of seas -
Yet still the blood is strong, the heart is Highland,
    And we in dreams behold the Hebrides.

We ne'er shall tread the fancy-haunted valley,
    Where 'tween the dark hills creeps the small clear stream,
In arms around the patriarch banner rally,
    Nor see the moon on royal tombstones gleam.

When the bold kindred, in the time long vanish'd,
    Conquer'd the soil and fortified the keep -
No seer foretold the children would be banish'd.
    That a degenerate lord might boast his sheep.

Come foreign rage - let Discord burst in slaughter!
    O then for clansmen true, and stern claymore
The hearts that would have given their blood like water,
    Beat heavily beyond the Atlantic roar.

*Anonymous*
*18th Century*

1  upland cottage

# In the Highlands

In the highlands, in the country places,
Where the old plain men have rosy faces,
And the young fair maidens
    Quiet eyes;
Where essential silence cheers and blesses,
And for ever in the hill-recesses
*Her* more lovely music
    Broods and dies.

O to mount again where erst I haunted;
Where the old red hills are bird-enchanted,
And the low green meadows
    Bright with sward;

And when even dies, the million-tinted,
And the night has come, and planets glinted,
Lo, the valley hollow
    Lamp-bestarred!

O to dream, O to wake and wander
There, and with delight to take and render,
Through the trance of silence
    Quiet breath;
Lo! for there, among the flowers and grasses,
Only the mightier movement sounds and passes;
Only winds and river,
    Life and death.

*Robert Louis Stevenson*
*1850-1894*

# Lyric from 'The Crier by Night'

The bird in my heart's a-calling through a far-fled, tear-grey sea
To the soft slow hills that cherish dim waters weary for me,
Where the folk of rath and dun trail homeward silently
In the mist of the early night-fall that drips from their hair like rain.

The bird in my heart's a-flutter, for the bitter wind of the sea
Shivers with thyme and woodbine as my body with memory;
I feel their perfumes ooze in my ears like melody -
The scent of the mead at the harping I shall not hear again.

The bird in my heart's a-sinking to a hushed vale hid in the sea,
Where the moonlit dew o'er dead fighters is stirred by the feet of the
                                                    Shee,
Who are lovely and old as the earth but younger than I can be
Who have known the forgetting of dying to a life one lonely pain.

*Gordon Bottomley*
*19th Century*

# The Dreary Change

The sun upon the Weirdlaw Hill,
    In Ettrick's vale, is sinking sweet;
The westland wind is hush and still,
    The lake lies sleeping at my feet.
Yet not the landscape to mine eye
    Bears those bright hues that once it bore;
Though evening, with her richest dye,
    Flames o'er the hills of Ettrick's shore.

With listless look along the plain
    I see Tweed's silver current glide,
And coldly mark the holy fane
    Of Melrose rise in ruin'd pride.
The quiet lake, the balmy air,
    The hill, the stream, the tower, the tree, -
Are they still such as once they were,
    Or is it the dreary change in me?

Alas, the warp'd and broken board,
    How can it bear the painter's dye!
The harp of strain'd and tuneless chord,
    How to the minstrel's skill reply!
To aching eyes each landscape lowers,
    To feverish pulse each gale blows chill;
And Araby's or Eden's bowers
    Were barren as this moorland hill.

*Sir Walter Scott*
*1771-1832*

# My Heart's in the Highlands

My heart's in the Highlands, my heart is not here;
My heart's in the Highlands a chasing the deer;
Chasing the wild deer, and following the roe;
My heart's in the Highlands, wherever I go.

Farewell to the Highlands, farewell to the North;
The birth-place of valour, the country of worth:
Wherever I wander, wherever I rove,
The hills of the Highlands for ever I love.

Farewell to the mountains high cover'd with snow;
Farewell to the Straths and green valleys below:
Farewell to the forests and wild-hanging woods;
Farewell to the torrents and loud-pouring floods.

My heart's in the Highlands, my heart is not here,
My heart's in the Highlands a chasing the deer:
Chasing the wild deer, and following the roe;
My heart's in the Highlands, wherever I go.

*Robert Burns*
*1759-1796*

# A Kiss of the King's Hand

It wasna from a golden throne,
Or a bower with milk-white roses blown,
But mid the kelp on northern sand
That I got a kiss of the King's hand.

I durstna raise my een to see
If he even cared to glance at me;
His princely brow with care was crossed
For his true men slain and kingdom lost.

Think not his hand was soft and white,
Or his fingers a' with jewels dight,
Or round his wrists were ruffles grand
When I got a kiss of the King's hand.

But dearer far to my twa een
Was the ragged sleeve of red and green
O'er that young weary hand that fain,
With the guid broadsword, had found its ain.

Farewell for ever, the distance grey
And the lapping ocean seemed to say -
For him a home in a foreign land.
And for me one kiss of the King's hand.

*Sarah Robertson Matheson*
*poem appeared 1894*

# Go, Hart, Unto the Lamp of Licht

Go, hart, unto the lamp of licht.
    Go, hart, do service and honour,
Go, hart, and serve him day and nicht:
    Go, hart, unto thy Saviour.

Go, hart, to thy onlie remeid
    Descending from the hevinlie tour,
Thee to deliver from pain and deid;
    Go, hart, unto thy Saviour.

Go, hart, but[1] dissimulatioun,
    To Christ that tuke our wild nature
For thee to suffer passioun;
    Go, hart, unto thy Saviour.

Go, hart, richt humill and meek,
    Go, hart, as leil[2] and trew servitour
To him that heil[3] is for all seick;
    Go, hart, unto thy Saviour.

Go, hart, with trew and hail intent
    To Christ, thy help and hail succour;
Thee to redeem, He was all rent;
    Go, hart, unto thy Saviour.

To Christ, that raise from deith to live,
    Go, hart, unto my latter hour;
Whase great mercy can nane descrive;[4]
    Go, hart, unto thy Saviour.

*Anonymous*

1 without
2 trusty
3 healing
4 describe

# Auld Lang Syne

Should auld acquaintance be forgot,
    And never brought to mind?
Should auld acquaintance be forgot
    And days o'lang syne?[1]

For auld lang syne, my jo,[2]
    For auld lang syne,
We'll tak a cup o' kindness yet
    For auld lang syne.

And surely you'll be your pint-stowp,[3]
    And surely I'll be mine,
And we'll tak a cup o' kindness yet
    For auld lang syne!

    For auld lang syne, etc

We twa hae run about the braes,
    And pu'd the gowans[4] fine,
But we've wander'd monie a weary fit[5]
    Sin' auld lang syne.

    For auld lang syne, etc

We twa hae paidl'd in the burn
    Frae morning sin til dine,
But seas between us braid[6] hae roar'd
    Sin' auld lang syne.

    For auld lang syne, etc

And there's a hand, my trusty fiere,
    And gie's a hand of thine,
And we'll tak a right guid-willie waught[7]
    For auld lang syne!

    For auld lang syne, etc

*Robert Burns*
*1759-1796*

1 former days
2 dear
3 tankard
4 daisies
5 foot
6 broad
7 friendly draught

# Extract from 'The Dream of the World Without Death'

' I laid my little girl upon a wood-bier,
And very sweet she seemed, and near unto me;
And slipping flowers into her shroud was comfort.

I put my silver mother in the darkness,
And kissed her, and was solaced by her kisses,
And set a stone, to mark the place, above her.

And green, green were their quiet sleeping places,
So green that it was pleasant to remember
That I and my tall man would sleep beside them.

The closing of dead eyelids is not dreadful,
For comfort comes upon us when we close them,
And tears fall, and our sorrow grows familiar;

And we can sit above them where they slumber,
And spin a dreamy pain into a sweetness,
And know instead that we are very near to them.'

*Robert Buchanan*
*born 1841*

# Ettrick Forest in November

November's sky is chill and drear,
November's leaf is red and sear:
Late, gazing down the steepy linn,
That hems our little garden in,
Low in its dark and narrow glen
You scarce the rivulet might ken,
So thick the tangled greenwood grew,
So feeble trill'd the streamlet through:
Now, murmuring hoarse, and frequent seen
Through bush and brier, no longer green,
An angry brook, it sweeps the glade,
Brawls over rock and wild cascade,
And, foaming brown with doubled speed,
Hurries its waters to the Tweed.

No longer Autumn's glowing red
Upon our Forest hills is shed;
No more beneath the evening beam
Fair Tweed reflects their purple gleam;

Away hath pass'd the heather-bell
That bloom'd so rich on Needpathfell;
Sallow his brow; and russet bare
Are now the sister-heights of Yair.
The sheep, before the pinching heaven,
To shelter'd dale and down are driven,
Where yet some faded herbage pines,
And yet a watery sunbeam shines:
In meek despondency they eye
The wither'd sward and wintry sky,
And far beneath their summer hill,
Stray sadly by Glenkinnon's rill:
The shepherd shifts his mantle's fold,
And wraps him closer from the cold;
His dogs no merry circles wheel,
But shivering follow at his heel;
A cowering glance they often cast,
As deeper moans the gathering blast.

*Sir Walter Scott 1771-1832*

# Romance

I will make you brooches and toys for your delight
Of bird-song at morning and star-shine at night.
I will make a palace fit for you and me,
Of green days in forests and blue days at sea.


I will make my kitchen, and you shall keep your room,
Where white flows the river and bright blows the broom,
And you shall wash your linen and keep your body white
In rainfall at morning and dewfall at night.


And this shall be for music when no one else is near,
The fine song for singing, the rare song to hear!
That only I remember, that only you admire,
Of the broad road that stretches and the roadside fire.


*Robert Louis Stevenson*
*1850-1894*

# Tam I' The Kirk

O Jean, my Jean, when the bell ca's the congregation,
Owre valley an' hill wi' the ding frae its iron mou',
When a' body's thochts is set on his ain salvation,
  Mine's set on you.

There's a reid rose lies on the Biuk o' the Word afore ye
That was growin' braw on its bush at the keek o' day,
But the lad that pu'd yon flower i' the mornin's glory
  He canna pray.

He canna pray; but there's nane i' the kirk will heed him
Whaur he sits his lane at the side o' the wa'.
For nane but the reid rose kens what my lassie gie'd him:
  It an' us twa!

He canna sing for the sang that his ain he'rt raises,
He canna see for the mist that's afore his een,
And a voice drouns the hale o' the psalms an' the paraphrases,
  Cryin' 'Jean, Jean, Jean!'

*Violet Jacob*
*1863-1946*

55

# The Coolun

Come with me, under my coat,
And we will drink our fill
Of the milk of the white goat,
Or wine if it be thy will;
And we will talk until
Talk is a trouble, too,
Out on the side of the hill,
And nothing is left to do,
But an eye to look into an eye
And a hand in a hand to slip,

And a sigh to answer a sigh,
And a lip to find out a lip:
What if the night be black
And the air on the mountain chill,
Where the goat lies down in her track
And all but the fern is still!
Stay with me under my coat,
And we will drink our fill
Of the milk of the white goat
Out on the side of the hill.

*James Stephens*
*19th Century*

# To the Sun

Greeting to you, sun of the seasons, as you travel the skies on high, with your strong steps on the wing of the heights; you are the happy mother of the stars.

You sink down in the perilous ocean without harm and without hurt, you rise up on the quiet wave like a young queen in flower.

*Scottish Gaelic; traditional folk prayer*

# Monaltri

There's a sound on the hill,
    Not of joy but of ailing;
Dark-hair'd women mourn -
    Beat their hands, with loud wailing.

They cry out, Ochon!
    For the young Monaltri,
Who went to the hill;
    But home came not he.

Without snood, without plaid
    Katrina's gone roaming.
O Katrina, my dear!
    Homeward be coming.

Och! hear, on the castle
    Yon pretty bird singing,
'Snoodless and plaidless,
    Her hands she is ringing.'

*Anonymous*

# My Own, my Native Land!

Breathes there the man with soul so dead,
Who never to himself hath said,
This is my own, my native land!
Whose heart hath ne'er within him burn'd
As home his footsteps he hath turn'd,
From wandering on a foreign strand!
If such there breathe, go, mark him well;
For him no minstrel raptures swell;
High though his titles, proud his name,
Boundless his wealth as wish can claim;
Despite these titles, power, and pelf,
The wretch, concentred all in self,
Living, shall forfeit fair renown,
And, doubly dying, shall go down
To the vile dust, from whence he sprung,
Unwept, unhonour'd, and unsung.

O Caledonia! stern and wild,
Meet a nurse for a poetic child!
Land of brown heath and shaggy wood,
Land of the mountain and the flood,
Land of my sires! what mortal hand
Can e'er untie the filial band
That knits me to thy rugged strand?
Still, as I view each well-known scene,
Think of what is now, and what hath been,
Seems as, to me, of all bereft,
Sole friends thy woods and streams were
left;
And this I love them better still,
Even in extremity of ill.

*Sir Walter Scott*
*1771-1832*

# Culloden Moor
## (Seen in Autumn Rain)

Full of grief, the low winds sweep
    O'er the sorrow-haunted ground;
Dark the woods where night rains weep,
    Dark the hills that watch around.

Tell me, can the joys of spring
    Ever make this sadness flee,
Make the woods with music ring,
    And the streamlet laugh for glee?

When the summer moor is lit
    With the pale fire of the broom,
And through green the shadows flit,
    Still shall mirth give place to gloom?

Sad shall it be, though sun be shed
    Golden bright on field and flood;
E'en the heather's crimson red
    Holds the memory of blood.

Here that broken, weary band
    Met the ruthless foe's array,
Where those moss-grown boulders stand,
    On that dark and fatal day.

Like a phantom hope had fled,
    Love to death was all in vain,
Vain, though heroes' blood was shed,
    And though hearts were broke in twain.

Many a voice has cursed the name
    Time has into darkness thrust,
Cruelty his only fame
    In forgetfulness and dust,

Noble dead that sleep below,
    We your valour ne'er forget;
Soft the heroes' rest who know
    Hearts like theirs are beating yet.

*Alice Macdonell*
*19th Century*

# Gin I was God

Gin I was God, sittin' up there abeen,[1]
Weariet nae doot noo a' my darg[2] was deen,[3]
Deaved[4] wie' the harps an' hymns oonendin' ringing,
Tired o' the flockin' angels hairse[5] wi' singin',
To some clood-edge I'd daunder[6] furth an', feth,
Look ower an' watch hoo things were gyaun[7] aneth.[8]
Syne,[9] gin[10] I saw hoo men I'd made mysel'
Had startit in to pooshan,[11] sheet[12] an' fell,
To reive[13] an' rape, an' fairly mak' a hell
O' my braw birlin' Earth, - a hale week's wark -
I'd cast my coat again, rowe up my sark,[14]
An', or they'd time to lench[15] a second ark,
Tak' bak my word an' sen' anither spate,
Droon oot the hale hypothec,[16] dicht[17] the sklate,[18]
Own my mistak', an' aince I'd cleared the brod,[19]
Start a' thing ower[20] again, gin I was God.

*Charles Murray*
*1864-1941*

| | |
|---|---|
| 1 above | 11 poison |
| 2 work | 12 shoot |
| 3 done | 13 harry |
| 4 deafened | 14 shirtsleeves |
| 5 hoarse | 15 launch |
| 6 wander | 16 thing |
| 7 going | 17 wipe |
| 8 beneath | 18 slate |
| 9 then | 19 board |
| 10 if, given | 20 over |